Mastering the Guitar Duets

William Bay and Mike Christiansen

To access the online audio recording of these duets go to:
WWW.MELBAY.COM/30873MEB

Visit us at www.melbay.com — E-mail us at email@melbay.com

Preface

The *Mastering the Guitar* series is a ground-breaking guitar method which combines a rich assortment of musical genres and teaches both playing with a pick and fingerstyle. Mike Christiansen and I authored and arranged 26 duets in that method. Over the years we have had requests to make those duets available in a separate book. This is a collection of those duets. The piece "Star in the Night" was expanded in my later duet book and recording titled "Acoustic Guitar Portraits". The expanded version of that duet is included here. These duets are fun to play and represent works in contemporary musical genres and by some great classical composers. The pieces are quite suitable as concert or recital selections and will supplement and enhance any guitar method.

William Bay

Contents

Bahía Tranquilo

First Guitar - solo; flatpick or fingerstyle
Second Guitar - accompaniment; fingerstyle

William Bay

Gentle, bossa nova feeling

1st
2nd

Em Em
Am7 F#°
Bm7 G B7♭9 Em
Am7 F#° Em B7♭9
Em B7♭9 Em F#m7-5 B7+5 Em

Reflection

Flatpick or Fingerstyle

Slow, dream like

William Bay

1st

2nd

Fma7 Bbma7 Fma7 Ami7

Gm7 C7sus Fma7 Bbma7

Fma7 Bb (C Bass) Fma7 Bbma7

Fma7 Ami7 Gmi7 C7sus Fma7

Bbma7 Fma7 Bbma7 Fma7 Fma7 (addD)

Sea of Glass

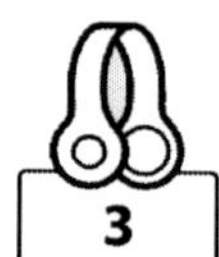

Flatpick or Fingerstyle

Slow, flowing tempo

William Bay

Reverie

Flatpick
Slowly

William Bay

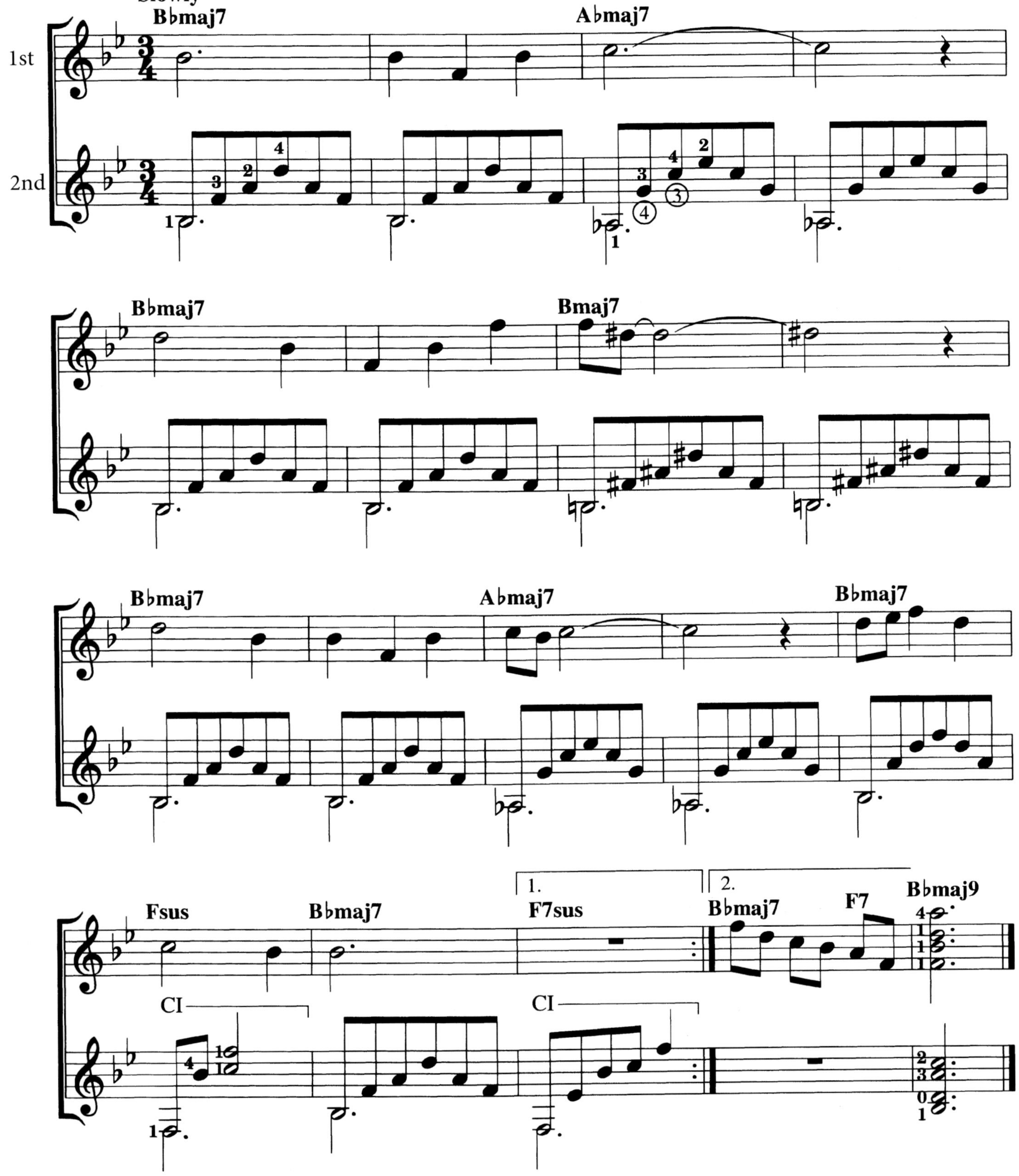

1st
2nd

B♭maj7 **A♭maj7**

B♭maj7 **Bmaj7**

B♭maj7 **A♭maj7** **B♭maj7**

Fsus **B♭maj7** 1. **F7sus** 2. **B♭maj7** **F7** **B♭maj9**

CI CI

Star in the Night

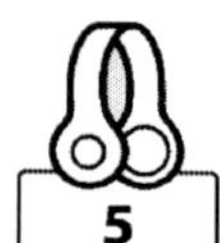

Flatpick
Dropped-D Tuning

William Bay

Adagio ♩. = 80

1st
2nd
mp
V pos
①

A

4
1
3
1
2
3
2
4
1

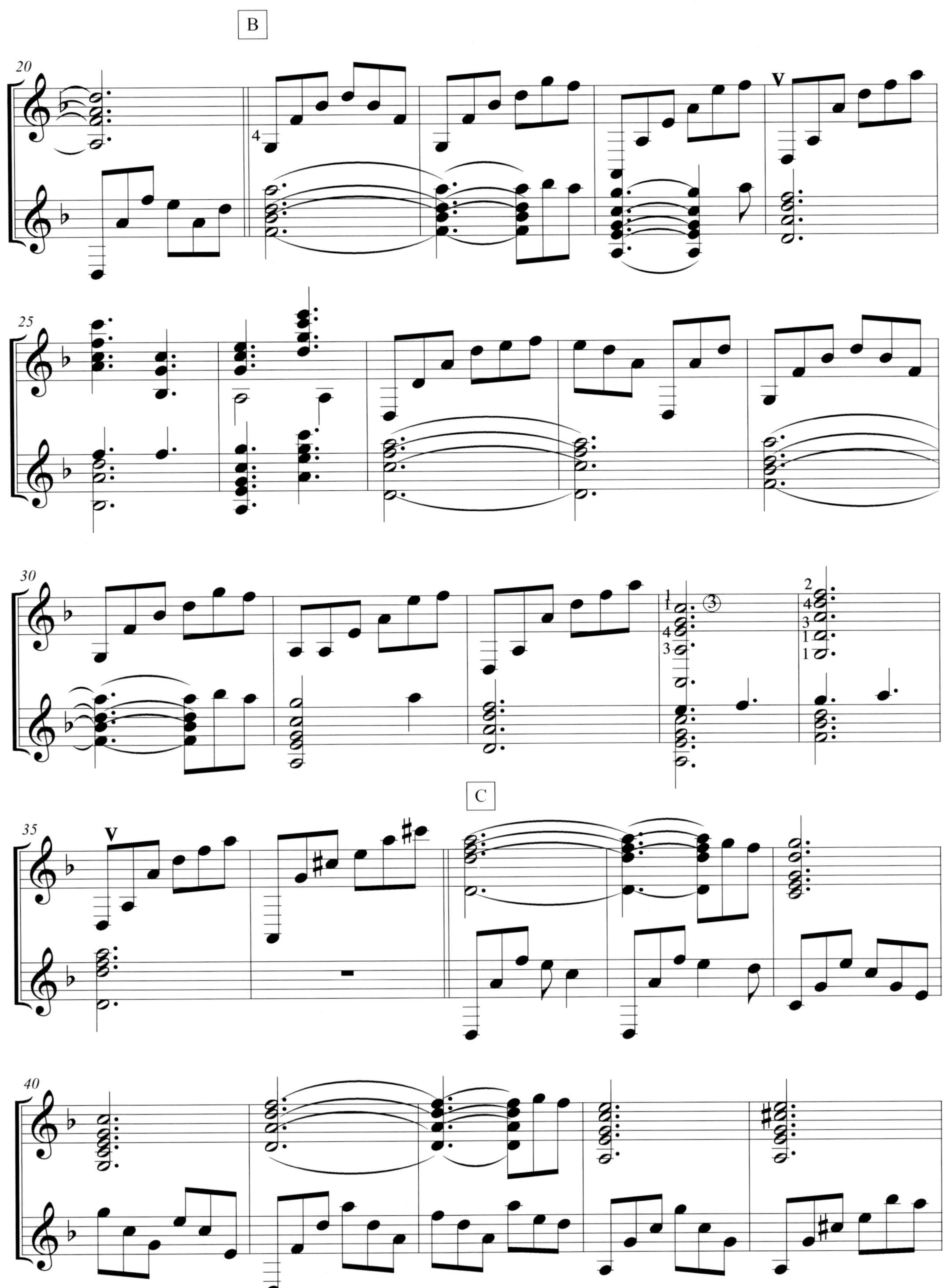
B
C

45
4
1
3
1
D
50
V pos
1
3
2
4
1
E
55
60
F
65
G
3

H
I
V

J
K

L
5

6
Jesu, Joy of Man's Desiring
Flatpick
Flowing ♩. = 66
William Bay
J. S. Bach
1st
2nd

Menuett

Mike Christiansen
G. P. Telemann

Flatpick or Fingerstyle

Fugue in D

8

Mike Christiansen
Fernando Carulli

Flatpick or Fingerstyle

♩ = 116

1st

2nd

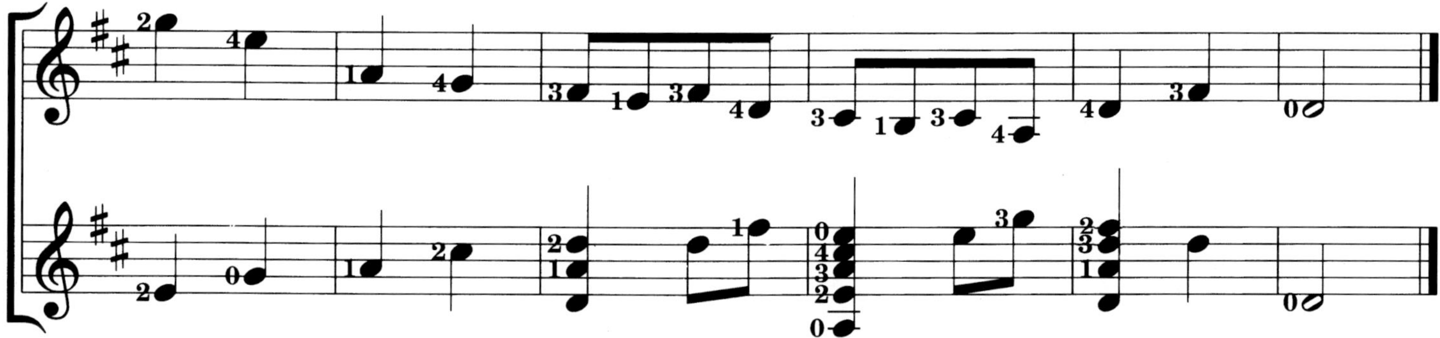

Autumn
Duet from *"The Four Seasons"*

First Guitar - flatpick or fingerstyle; standard tuning.
Second Guitar - flatpick or fingerstyle; Dropped-D tuning.

William Bay
Antonio Vivaldi

⑥ = D

Allegro ♩ = 88

1st
2nd

f
p
f
p

f
p
f
p
f
3
1
3
4
p
mf

Hornpipe
From "*Water Music*"

First Guitar - flatpick or fingerstyle.
Second Guitar - fingerstyle; Dropped-D tuning.

William Bay
Handel

⑥ = D **Moderately** 𝅗𝅥 **= 96**

1st
2nd

tr
f
mf
f
tr
mf
p
f
mf

f
mf
p
mf
tr
f
tr

Winter

From *"The Four Seasons"*

First Guitar - flatpick or fingerstyle; Dropped-D tuning
Second Guitar - fingerstyle; Dropped-D tuning

William Bay
Antonio Vivaldi

⑥ = D

Largo cantabile, very slowly ♩ = 44

1st

2nd

tr

tr
2
1
3
0
0
4
1
1
1
0
0

Preludio

12

First Guitar - flatpick or fingerstyle
Second Guitar - fingerstyle; Dropped-D tuning

William Bay
Corelli

tr

13

Bourée

From "Suite No. 2"

First Guitar - flatpick or fingerstyle
Second Guitar - fingerstyle

William Bay
J. S. Bach

Sarabande

William Bay
Corelli

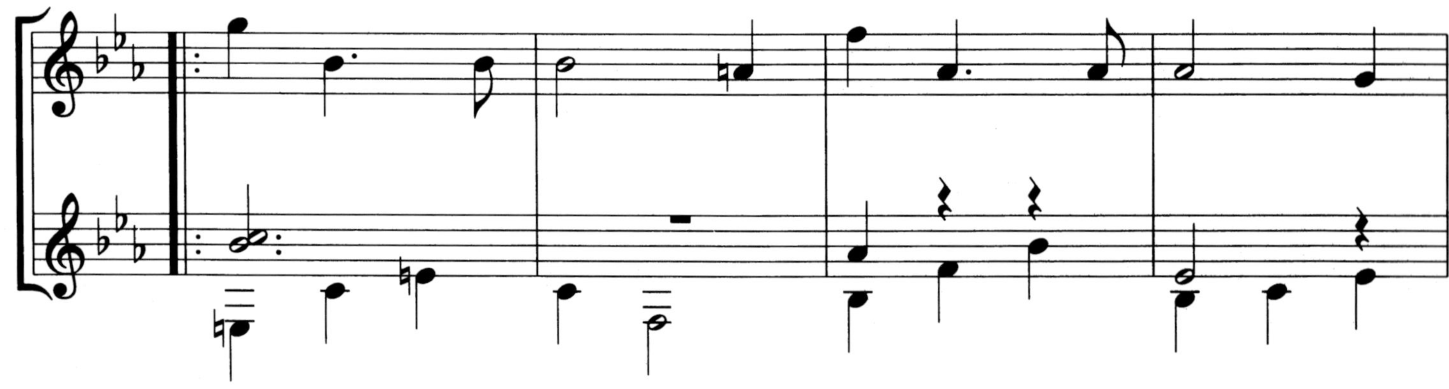

Hired Hands

Mike Christiansen

Gigue

From *"Sonata No. 9, Op. 5"*

William Bay
Corelli

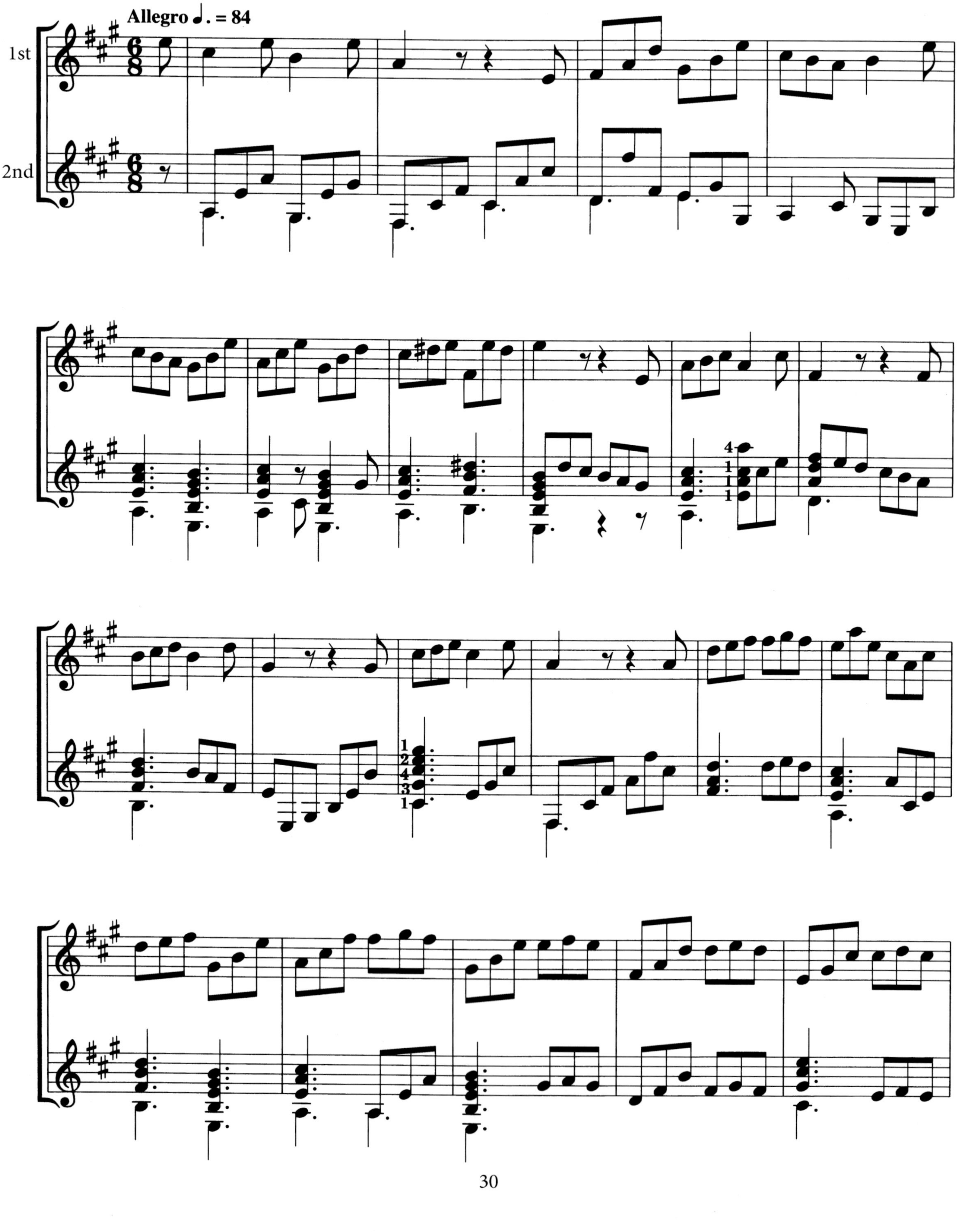

Allegro ♩. = 84

1st
2nd

To Coda
D.C. al Coda
Coda

Forest Flowers

First Guitar - flatpick or fingerstyle
Second Guitar - fingerstyle

William Bay
Finnish Folk Melody

Gavotte

William Bay
J. S. Bach

Flatpick

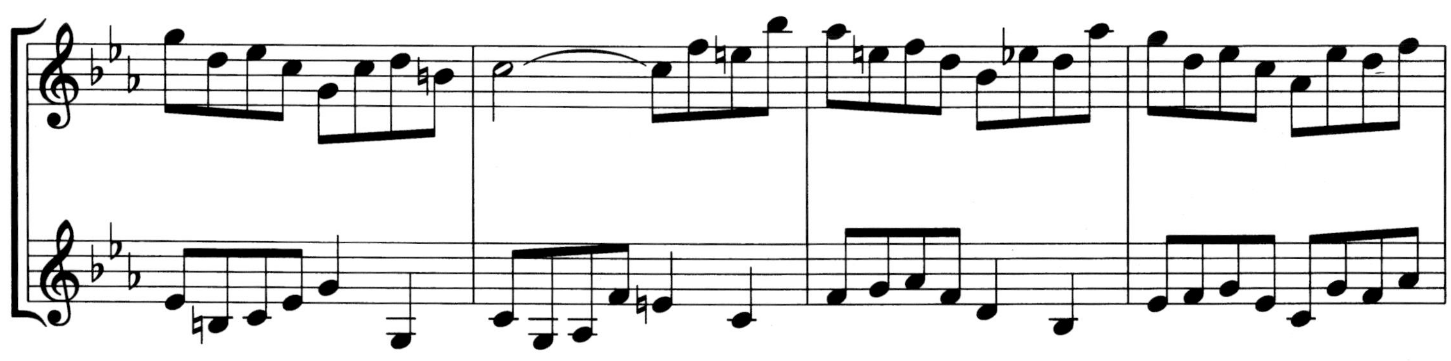

Sleeper's Wake

19

First Guitar - flatpick or fingerstyle
Second Guitar - fingerstyle

William Bay
J. S. Bach

tr
1.
2.

Rondeau

Mike Christiansen
J. P. Rameau

1.
2.

Email Special

Mike Christiansen

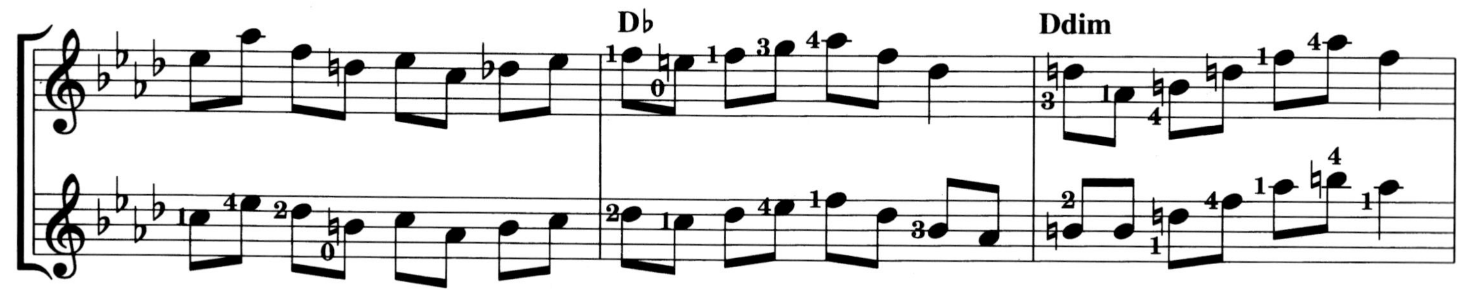

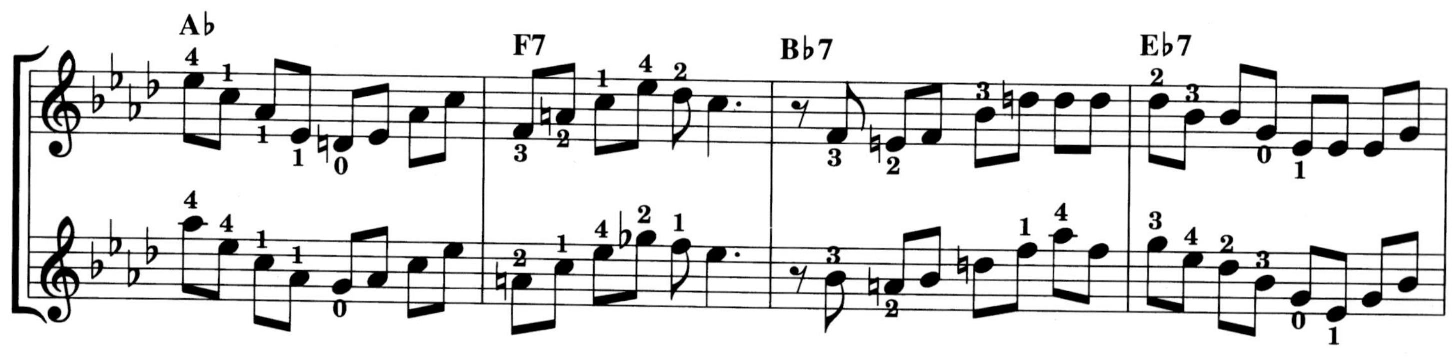

D♭
Ddim
A♭
F7
B♭7
E♭7
A♭
A7
A♭7

22
Largo
Mike Christiansen
Zipoli
Slowly, legato ♩ = 63
1st
2nd

Ortega

23

First Guitar - flatpick
Second Guitar - flatpick or fingerstyle

William Bay

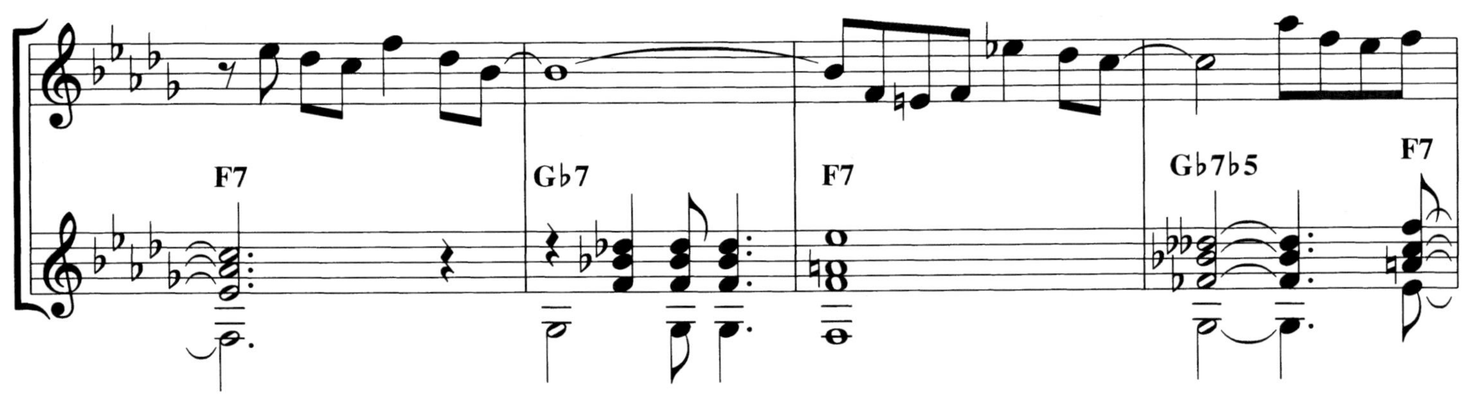
F7
Gb7
F7
Gb7b5
F7

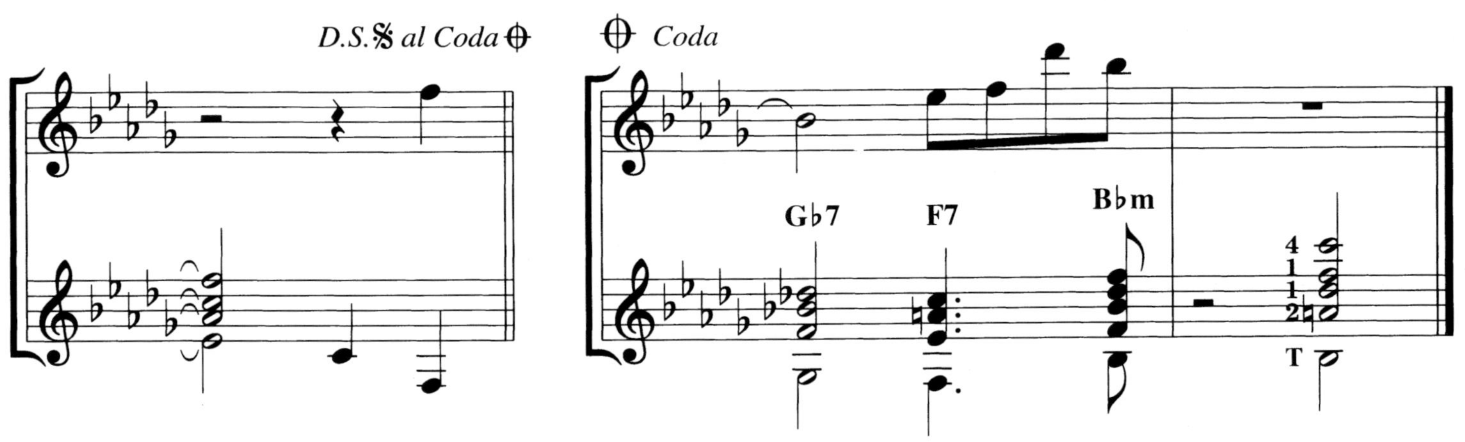
D.S. al Coda
Coda
Gb7
F7
Bbm
4
1
1
2
T

Pavanne

William Bay
16th Century
French Court Dance

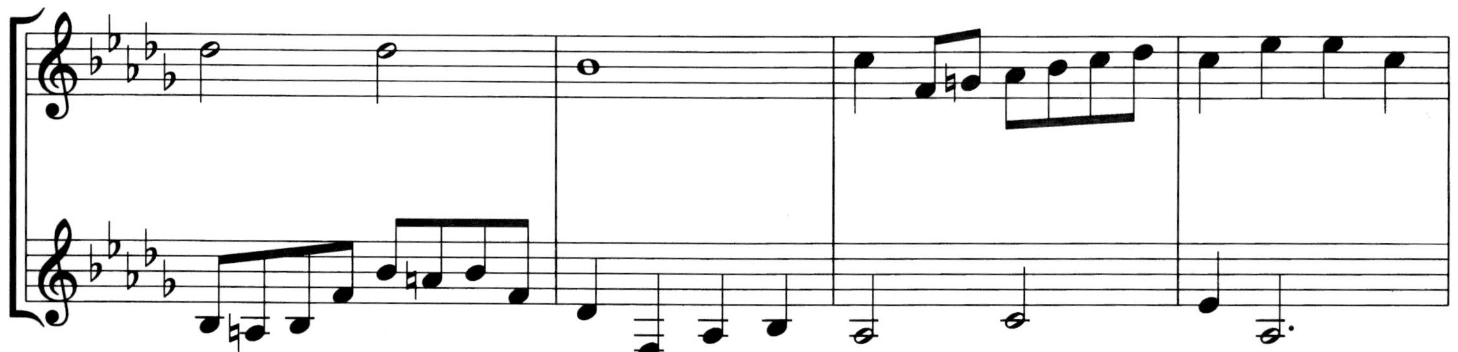

Galliarde

William Bay
16th Century
French Court Dance

ritard.

Invention in F Minor

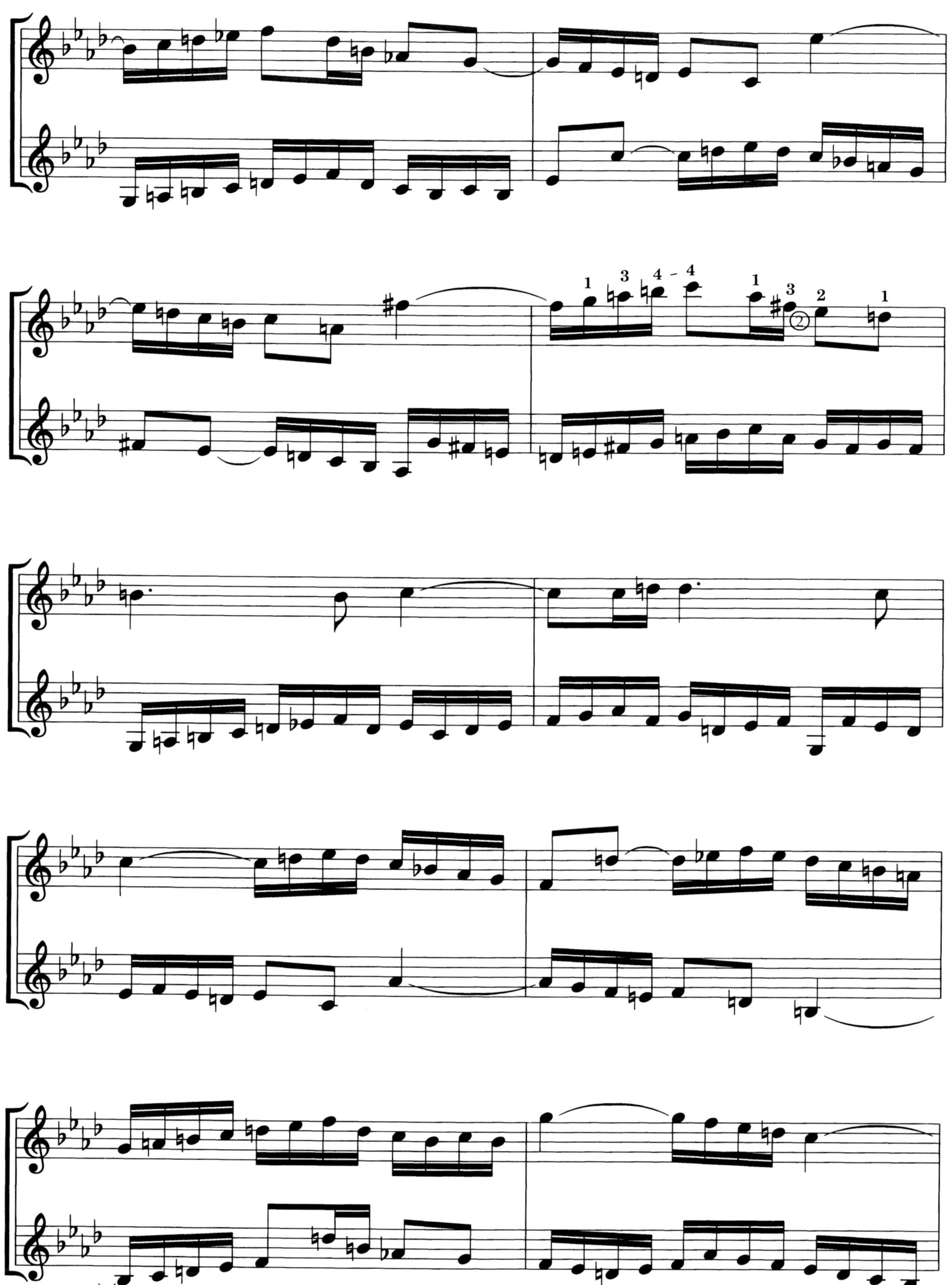
1 3 4 - 4 1 3 2 1
2

tr